MY FIRST
HANUKKAH BOOK

by Aileen Fisher
illustrated by Priscilla Kiedrowski

created by The Child's World

CHILDRENS PRESS ™

CHICAGO

Library of Congress Cataloging in Publication Data

Fisher, Aileen Lucia, 1906-
  My first Hanukkah book.

  Summary: Presents poems relating to Hanukkah—the
aspects of it that are fun and the memory of its origin.
    1. Hanukkah—Juvenile poetry.   2. Children's poetry,
American.   [1. Hanukkah—Poetry.   2. American poetry]
I. Kiedrowski, Priscilla, ill.   II. Child's World (Firm)
III. Title.
PS3511.I7294M9   1985   811'.52   84-21510
ISBN 0-516-02905-3

MY FIRST

HANUKKAH
BOOK

Year~End

The year is coming
to an end
with dark and wintry nights.
But, oh, it brings us
Hanukkah,
the Festival of Lights!

Eight Days

Hanukkah's a happy time,
bringing family fun.
It lasts not one, but
eight full days, with treats,
and games to play
and gifts for everyone.

All Together

If winter snow is grimy gray
or fluffy as a feather,
Hanukkah's a happy time. . .
with all of us together.

Treats

Orange-flavored doughnuts
are treats of which I dream.
But though they're very special,
they're never as supreme
as small potato pancakes,
hot potato pancakes,
crisp potato pancakes,
with applesauce and cream.

Spin the Dreidel

Spin the dreidel!* When it slows,
speak the letter that it shows:

נ (nun) — get nothing from the pot.
ה (heh) — get half (perhaps a lot).
ש (shin) — put one more token in.
ג (gimmel) — get all from the pot,
perhaps a little,
perhaps a lot.

*Dreidel is a top with a Hebrew letter
on each side. Pronounced dray-dul.

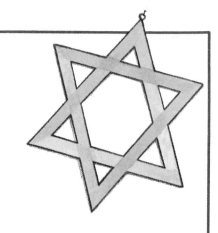

Hanukkah Fun

Spin your dreidel
round and round.
It makes you feel so merry.
Spin yourself
around, around,
just like a dancing fairy.

Menorah

Colored candles,
twisted, small—
Hanukkah
needs eight in all.

One the first night.
Next night, two.
Next night, three. . .
until you're through.

Light them,
put all eight, aglow,
in the window
where they'll show.

Candlelight

Candlelight for Hanukkah
as the year grows older!
One new candle every night
in a polished holder,
standing for a noble past,
a free-to-worship story,
as the candles, eight* in all,
stand in shining glory.

*(The ninth candle is the
lighting candle called the
Shamash.)

19

History

At Hanukkah
the candlelight
reminds us
of the brave, brave fight
in years gone by
to win the right
to have our temple
and to pray
to our one God
in our own way.

Remembering

Time now for remembering
as well as having fun.
Remembering with thankfulness
the battle that was won.
Fun to light the candlewicks
as soon as day is done. . . .
Time now for remembering
as well as having fun.

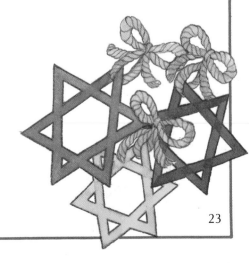

Spelldown

H for home and holiday,
A for all to sing and play,
N for nights when candles glow
    in the window, on the snow.
U for using tops to spin,
K for kindness,
K for kin.
A for acting proud and gay,
H for happy holiday.

Hanukkah Gelt

Sometimes our gift is money
called gelt . . . all shiny new.
We're fond of such a present—
a lot of coins, or few.
*Some*times in shiny wrappers
surprises greet us, too:
our gelt is made of chocolate. . .
and we know what to do!

Hanukkah Candles

A candle for the songs we sing,
for gifts,
for games we play,
for crisp potato pancakes on a
    happy holiday,
for stories,
and for heroes like Judah
    Maccabee,
for battles won so long ago
that finally made us free
to pray in our own way
on this and every day.

Miracle of Lights

"We won the right," the people cried,
"to pray *our* way. But where's the
oil to make a light? Each jar was
broken in the fight."

They found a jar with oil to pour
in *one* small holder, nothing more.

The lighted wick burned all night through,
and then the oil made fuel for *two*,
two nights, then three; the next night, four,
with shadows on the Temple floor. . .
for eight full nights the light burned clear—
a miracle that far off year
when Hanukkah was born!